The Gate of your Life

By

Dr. D. K. Olukoya

The Gate of your Life

A publication of
MOUNTAIN OF FIRE AND MIRACLES MINISTRIES
13, Olasimbo Street, off Olumo Road, Onike,
P. O. Box 2990, Sabo, Yaba, Lagos, Nigeria.

ISBN: 978-978-8424-51-2

For further information or permission contact:
Email: pasteurdanielolukoya_french@yahoo.fr
mfmhqworldwide@mountainoffire.org

Or visit our website: www.mountainoffire.org
http://mfmbiligualbooks4evangelism.blogspot.com/

We are looking at the topic entitled, *"The gate of your life."*

Genesis 28:12 says, "And he dreamed, and behold a ladder set up on the earth, and the top of it reached to heaven: and behold the angels of God ascending and descending on it."

According to the verse in the foregoing, Jacob saw a ladder set up on the earth, the top of it reached the heaven and the angels of the Lord were ascending and descending on it. Verse 13 says, "And, behold, the Lord stood above it, and said, I am the Lord God of Abraham thy father, and the God of Isaac; the land wherein thou liest, to thee will I give it, and to thy seed."

Beloved, before you read further, I would like you to talk to the Lord: "Every land that belongs to me, that is presently in the hand of the enemy I recover it by fire, in the name of Jesus."

Verses 16-17 say, "And Jacob awaked out of his sleep, and he said, surely the Lord is in this place, and I knew it not. And he was afraid, and said, how dreadful this place is! This is none other but the house of God, and this is the gate of heaven."

Matthew 16:18-19 says, "And I say also unto thee, that thou art Peter, and upon this rock I will build my church: and the gates of hell shall not prevail against it."

WHAT IS A GATE?

A gate is a very important part of a building or house. A gate is for security and protection. In the Bible, the gate was a focal point of power. Business was conducted at the gate. Military strategy was planned at the gate. Judgment and punishments were delivered at the gate. The Bible says, "The husband of a virtuous woman was known at the gate" (Proverbs 31:23). Abraham's Nephew, Lot sat at the gate of Sodom as an elder. So, in ancient times, gates were very important because the safety of a city was determined by the strength of the gate. If the enemy stormed the gate and succeeded, the horses and chariots of war would enter into it. So, when the gate came down, the city was conquered.

TYPES OF GATES

There are physical gates and there are spiritual gates. There are visible and invisible gates. A gate is an opening in a wall or fence. It is an opening in a city or house. And normally it is built with defensive structures. It is a means of entrance or exit. It is an area of departure or arrival. A gate is a door or any mechanism for controlling passage. Just as physical gates and spiritual gates have their own important values, there are gates that lead to the city of a person's life.

These truths are sometimes not clear to us. But the truth is clear to the children of darkness. Everyone has what is known as human gates through which the enemy can go in or come out. When the enemy has gained entrance and is already inside but you are fighting an external enemy, you are writing express letter to defeat. Many people are fighting the enemy outside when the enemy has already entered inside. Before you deal with the external enemy, you must deal with the internal one. There are nine major gates that open up the life of a man.

THE MAJOR GATES THAT OPEN UP THE LIFE OF A MAN

1. The head gate: The Bible says, "Lay hands suddenly on no man, so that you will not be a partaker of his iniquity" (1 Timothy 5:22). Generally, people pray for others while laying hands on their heads. Likewise people are generally anointed on the head. The Bible says, "Thou anointest my head with oil; my cup runneth over" (Psalm 23:5). The head is a means through which anointing is imparted into the body. The head is an access route to the anointing. A holy man of God can lay hands on you and the anointing of God will fall upon you and you will receive the baptism of the Holy Ghost. That head is the symbol of your destiny. Negative or positive anointing can flow through your head to the rest of your body. A lot of people have been attacked through the head gate. And if you are passing through this kind of trouble, you may be noticing memory loss; you are no longer as sharp as you used to be. You may find that you are forgetting what you should not forget. You may find sinning and all kinds of other negative things going on inside

the head. You may find that you are becoming sick and sick always. You may discover that any where you go, bad luck follows you, because the gate of the head has permitted something to enter. Remember the head is the symbol of your destiny. You can cut off a person's leg and the person will still survive. I have even seen somebody that has no hands and legs still living. But I have not seen a person who has no head still alive. So, you have to be careful, who lays hands on your head. You have to be careful, who puts hands on your head. Before many people got born again they have had evil hands laid on their heads. Many people too have poured all kinds of thing on their heads. Many have shaven their heads because of the dead. Many have incisions on their heads. Many have used their heads to carry sacrifices. Many have put all kinds of negative things on their heads. Many have been careless with their hair; the enemy has cut their hair away and has polluted it. Remember your head is the storehouse of your brain and this can be manipulated. That is why deliverance of the head is a serious matter.

2. The gate of the eyes: The eye gives light to the entire body. Your eyes can push you to hell fire. Jesus said if your eyes would make you go to hell fire, you better pluck it out. It is better to go to heaven blind than for you to have eyes and go to hell fire. Job said, "I have made a covenant with my eyes..." You should be careful what you behold. The eyes are like the lens of a camera. It takes pictures and transfers the image to your spirit man. The eye is therefore a major spiritual gate that can receive both positive and negative messages. Messages from the eyes are so quick to transfer because they are closer to the brain. For example, lust enters into the body through the eyes. There are some people who see negative things that others do not see. These things enter into their spirit man and cause trouble for them. Lay your hands on your eyes and pray like this: "Every spiritual padlock assigned against my eyes, die, in the name of Jesus."

3. The ear gate: Hearing comes through the ear gate. The Bible says, "Faith cometh by hearing, and hearing by the word of God." The reverse is also true. Doubt too can come by hearing and hearing the voice of the enemy. A person's spiritual ears may be blocked and he cannot receive information from heaven. You may pray and as you are praying, your ear is tinkling and you cannot hear anything. It means that God wants to speak to you but there is blockage in your ears. The enemy can programme somebody's ears to be receiving satanic messages. I pray that if the enemy has taken over your ear gate, you shall receive deliverance, in the name of Jesus.

4. The mouth gate: The mouth gate is dangerous in two ways. The mouth has a big fish swimming inside it. That big fish is called the tongue. If the word you speak are terrible, it means the enemy is using your mouth gate against you. Beloved, I want you to know this very well: We live on words and we die on words. We grow on words and we disintegrate on words. If you get a degree from a university, you got the degree because of the word of a teacher. The mouth gate does a daily destruction.

Your mouth can kill or make alive. That is the first danger. The second danger is the food you put in the mouth. The mouth gate put our forefathers Adam and Eve in trouble. A lot of people have taken concoctions, they ate what they should not eat and it has put them in trouble. I decree that any problem that has entered into your life through the mouth gate shall die, in the name of Jesus.

5. The gate of the hand: Your hand is the symbol of your labour. The Bible says, "God can teach your hands to war and your fingers to battle." Some people complain that they find cobwebs on their hands in their dreams. It means that the enemy is attacking the works of their hands. Evil can come to a person through the hand. The enemy can give you an evil handshake and spoil the works of your hands. I decree by the decree of God that any arrow fired into your hands to remove your prosperity shall go back to the sender, in the name of Jesus.

6. The heart gate: The heart is the control room of power. It is a bank, a storehouse of good and bad things. Once Satan gains access into the heart, all other departments of one's life will collapse. Evil thoughts and evil imaginations generate from the heart. The heart gate has destroyed so many people.

7. The navel gate: This is where you had connection to your mother for supplies when you were in the womb. It is the gate where evil blood, evil spirits and evil inheritance can pass into a child. Many people suffer today because of inherited problem. Many had their placentas manipulated. Many need to carry out personal deliverance on their navels. You can pray that any evil thing that has entered into your life through the navel should be destroyed in the name of Jesus.

8. The sex gate: The sex gate is the most successful gate used by Satan. There is practically nothing the enemy cannot do to the destiny of a person who is sexually loose. The enemy has destroyed so many useful destinies through this avenue. Demons and satanic materials can be programmed into a person

through the sex gate. Once you engage in sex outside marriage, you open a door to the enemy. This is why so many young men are not doing well. The enemy has already gained access to their lives. However, if you are a victim, you can pray for deliverance and the Lord will deliver you.

9. The gate of the legs: Your legs are the symbol of walking. Therefore, you must be careful where your legs take you to. If they had done satanic feet washing for you or you have put beads or chains on your legs or you stepped on charms or evil people picked dust from your feet, the enemy can gain access through your legs. There are many people that have cursed feet. Your feet are supposed to establish your dominion in the garden of your destiny, but if it is not able to do that and you are always walking into trouble, you need to pray against it today. I know a man; as he was going to work one morning, he did not look quite carefully. He just found that something hot was swelling on his legs, by the time he would look; he found that he had dipped his right leg into a *pot of sacrifice* and beginning from that day his life was upside down. You can pray that you shall travel the map of your destiny, in the name of Jesus. You can also decree that your legs will bring you into uncommon breakthroughs, in the name of Jesus.

HOW TO DEAL WITH THE PROBLEMS OF THE GATES

1. Surrender your life to Jesus.
2. Repent of every known sin.
3. Send out the strangers that have already gained access to your life.
4. Remove the property of the strangers that has been dwelling inside your life.
5. Barricade your life and set a watch over your gates so that the enemy does not gain access again, so that affliction will not rise again.

To deal with the problems of the gates of your life and to receive deliverance from the influx of the enemy into the gates of your life, you need to give your life to Christ if you have not done so. If you are ready to surrender your life to Jesus, make the following confession: "Lord Jesus, I come before you now. I surrender my life to you. I know that I am a sinner. Forgive me and wash me with your precious blood. Take absolute control of my life. Thank you Lord Jesus, in Jesus' name. Amen."

PRAYER POINTS

1. (Lay your right hand upon your head). Every power of my father's house that does not want me to lift my head, die, in the name of Jesus.
2. Lift up your right hand to the heavenlies and declare this: Every power that has stolen from me, I recover what you have stolen, in the name of Jesus.
3. Thou power of wickedness assigned against my breakthrough, your time is up, die, in the name of Jesus.

ABOUT D. K. OLUKOYA

Dr. D. K. Olukoya is the General Overseer of the Mountain of Fire and Miracles Ministries and the Battle Cry Ministries. He holds a First Class Honours Degree in Microbiology from the University of Lagos, Nigeria and a Ph.D. in Molecular Genetics from the University of Reading, United Kingdom. As a researcher, he has over eighty scientific publications to his credit. Anointed by God, Dr. Olukoya is a teacher, prophet, evangelist and preacher of the word. His life and that of his wife, Shade and their son, Elijah Toluwani, are living proofs that all power belongs to God.

ABOUT MOUNTAIN OF FIRE AND MIRACLES MINISTRIES

Mountain of Fire and Miracles Ministries, is a ministry devoted to the revival of apostolic signs, Holy Ghost fireworks and the unlimited demonstration of the power of God to deliver to the uttermost. Absolute holiness within and without, as the greatest spiritual insecticide, and a condition for heaven is taught openly. MFM is a do-it-yourself Gospel Ministry, where your hands are trained to wage war and your fingers to fight.

A brief history of Mountain of Fire and Miracles Ministries Incorporated

The Mountain of Fire and Miracles was founded in 1989. The first meeting was held at the home of Dr. D. K Olukoya and had 24 persons in attendance. The Church later moved to No. 60, Old Yaba Road, Lagos, and then to the present International Headquarters, site on 24th April, 1994. The Mountain of Fire and Miracles Ministries' Headquarters is the largest single Christian congregation in Africa, with attendance of over 200,000 in single meetings. Mountain of Fire and Miracles Ministries is a full gospel ministry devoted to the revival of apostolic signs, Holy Ghost fireworks and the unlimited demonstration of the power of God to deliver to the uttermost. Absolute holiness, within and without, as the greatest spiritual insecticide and a pre-requisite for heaven is taught openly. MFM is a do-it-yourself Gospel ministry, where your hands are trained to wage war and your fingers to do battle.

1. 20 Marching Orders To Fulfill Your Destiny
2. 30 Prophetic Arrows From Heaven
3. 30 Things The Anointing Can Do For You
4. Abraham's Children in Bondage
5. A-Z of Complete Deliverance
6. Basic Prayer Patterns
7. Be Prepared
8. Bewitchment must Die
9. Biblical Principles of Dream Interpretation
10. Born Great, But Tied Down
11. Breaking Bad Habits
12. Breakthrough Prayers For Business Professionals
13. Bringing Down The Power of God
14. Brokenness
15. Can God Trust You?
16. Command The Morning
17. Connecting to The God of Breakthroughs
18. Consecration Commitment & Loyalty
19. Contending For The Kingdom
20. Criminals In The House Of God
21. Dancers At The Gate of Death
22. Dealing Destiny Vultures
23. Dealing With Destiny Thieves
24. Dealing With Hidden Curses
25. Dealing With Local Satanic Technology
26. Dealing With Satanic Exchange
27. Dealing With The Evil Powers Of Your Father's House

28. Dealing With Tropical Demons
29. Dealing With Unprofitable Roots
30. Dealing With Witchcraft Barbers
31. Deep Secrets, Deep Deliverance
32. Deliverance By Fire
33. Deliverance From Evil Foundation
34. Deliverance From Spirit Husband And Spirit Wife
35. Deliverance From The Limiting Powers
36. Deliverance of The Brain
37. Deliverance Of The Conscience
38. Deliverance Of The Head
39. Deliverance of The Tongue
40. Deliverance: God's Medicine Bottle
41. Destiny Clinic
42. Destroying Satanic Masks
43. Disgracing Soul Hunters
44. Divine Military Training
45. Divine Prescription For Your Total Immunity
46. Divine Yellow Card
47. Dominion Prosperity
48. Drawers Of Power From The Heavenlies
49. Evil Appetite
50. Evil Umbrella
51. Facing Both Ways
52. Failure In The School Of Prayer
53. Fire For Life's Journey
54. For We Wrestle ...

55. Freedom Indeed
56. God's Key To A Happy Life
57. Healing Through Prayers
58. Holiness Unto The Lord
59. Holy Cry
60. Holy Fever
61. Hour Of Decision
62. How To Obtain Personal Deliverance
63. How To Pray When Surrounded By The Enemies
64. I Am Moving Forward
65. Idols Of The Heart
66. Igniting Your Inner Fire
67. Is This What They Died For?
68. Kill Your Goliath By Fire
69. Killing The Serpent of Frustration
70. Let Fire Fall
71. Let God Answer By Fire
72. Limiting God
73. Lord, Behold Their Threatening
74. Madness of The Heart
75. Making Your Way Through The Traffic Jam of Life
76. Meat For Champions
77. Medicine For Winners
78. My Burden For The Church
79. Open Heavens Through Holy Disturbance
80. Overpowering Witchcraft
81. Paralysing The Riders And The Horse

82. Personal Spiritual Check-Up
83. Possessing The Tongue of Fire
84. Power Against Coffin Spirits
85. Power Against Destiny Quenchers
86. Power Against Dream Criminals
87. Power Against Local Wickedness
88. Power Against Marine Spirits
89. Power Against Spiritual Terrorists
90. Power Against The Mystery of Wickedness
91. Power Against Unclean Spirits
92. Power Must Change Hands
93. Power of Brokenness
94. Power To Disgrace The Oppressors
95. Power To Recover Your Birthright
96. Power To Recover Your Lost Glory
97. Power To Shut Satanic Doors
98. Pray Your Way To Breakthroughs
99. Prayer Strategies For Singles
100. Prayer Is The Battle
101. Prayer Rain
102. Prayer To Kill Enchantment
103. Prayer To Make You Fulfill Your Divine Destiny
104. Prayer Warfare Against 70 Mad Spirits
105. Prayers For Open Heavens
106. Prayers To Destroy Diseases And Infirmities
107. Prayers To Move From Minimum To Maximum
108. Praying Against Foundational Poverty

109. Praying Against The Spirit Of The Valley
110. Praying In The Storm
111. Praying To Destroy Satanic Roadblocks
112. Praying To Dismantle Witchcraft
113. Principles of Conclusive Prayers
114. Principles Of Prayer
115. Raiding The House of The Strongman
116. Release From Destructive Covenants
117. Revoking Evil Decrees
118. Safeguarding Your Home
119. Satanic Diversion Of The Black Race
120. Secrets of Spiritual Growth And Maturity
121. Setting The Covens Ablaze
122. Seventy Rules of Spiritual Warfare
123. Seventy Sermons To Preach To Your Destiny
124. Silencing The Birds Of Darkness
125. Slave Masters
126. Slaves Who Love Their Chains
127. Smite The Enemy And He Will Flee
128. Speaking Destruction Unto The Dark Rivers
129. Spiritual Education
130. Spiritual Growth And Maturity
131. Spiritual Warfare And The Home
132. Stop Them Before They Stop You
133. Strategic Praying
134. Strategy Of Warfare Praying
135. Students In The School Of Fear

136. Symptoms Of Witchcraft Attack
137. Taking The Battle To The Enemy's Gate
138. The Amazing Power of Faith
139. The Baptism of Fire
140. The Battle Against The Spirit Of Impossibility
141. The Chain Breaker
142. The Dinning Table Of Darkness
143. The Enemy Has Done This
144. The Evil Cry Of Your Family Idol
145. The Fire Of Revival
146. The Gateway To Spiritual Power
147. The Great Deliverance
148. The Hidden Viper
149. The Internal Stumbling Block
150. The Lord is A Man of War
151. The Mystery Of Mobile Curses
152. The Mystery Of The Mobile Temple
153. The Power of Aggressive Prayer Warriors
154. The Power of Priority
155. The Prayer Eagle
156. The Pursuit Of Success
157. The Scale of The Almighty
158. The School of Tribulation
159. The Seasons Of Life
160. The Secrets Of Greatness
161. The Serpentine Enemies
162. The Skeleton In Your Grandfather's Cupboard

163. The Slow Learners
164. The Snake In The Power House
165. The Spirit Of The Crab
166. The Star Hunters
167. The Star In Your Sky
168. The Terrible Agenda
169. The Tongue Trap
170. The Unconquerable Power
171. The University of Champions
172. The Unlimited God
173. The Vagabond Spirit
174. The Way Of Divine Encounter
175. The Wealth Transfer Agenda
176. Tied Down In The Spirits
177. Too Hot To Handle
178. Turnaround Breakthrough
179. Unprofitable Foundations
180. Victory Over Satanic Dreams
181. Victory Over Your Greatest Enemies
182. Violent Prayers Against Stubborn Situations
183. War At The Edge Of Breakthroughs
184. Wasted At The Market Square of Life
185. Wasting The Wasters
186. Wealth Must Change Hands
187. What You Must Know About The House Fellowship
188. When God Is Silent
189. When The Battle is from Home

190. When The Deliverer Need Deliverance
191. When The Enemy Hides
192. When Things Get Hard
193. When You Are Knocked Down
194. When You Are Under Attack
195. When You Need A Change
196. Where Is Your Faith?
197. While Men Slept
198. Woman! Thou Art Loosed.
199. Your Battle And Your Strategy
200. Your Foundation And Destiny
201. Your Mouth And Your Deliverance
202. Your Mouth And Your Warfare

YORUBA PUBLICATIONS

1. Adura Agbayori
2. Adura Ti Nsi Oke Ni' di
3. Ojo Adura

FRENCH PUBLICATIONS

1. Bilan Spirituel Personnel
2. Cantique Des Contiques
3. Commander Le Matin
4. Comment Recevior La Delivrance Du Mari Et Femme De Nuit
5. Cpmment Se Delivrer Soi-meme
6. Demanteler La Sorcellerie
7. En Finir Avec Les Forces Malefiques De La Maison De Ton Pere

8. Espirit De Vagabondage
9. Femme Tu Es Liberee
10. Frappez l'adversaire Et Il Fuira
11. L'etoile Dans Votre Ciel
12. La Deliverance De La Tete
13. La Deliverance: Le Flacon De Medicament Dieu
14. La Deviation Satanique De La Race Noire
15. Le Combat Spirituel Et Le Foyer
16. Le Mauvais Cri Des Idoles
17. Le Programme De Tranfert De Richesse
18. Les Étudiants A l'ecole De La Peur
19. Les Saisons De La Vie
20. Les Strategies De Prieres Pour Les Celibataires
21. Ne Grand Mais Lie
22. Pluie De Priere
23. Pouvoir Contre Les Demond Tropicaux
24. Povoir Contre Les Terrorites Spirituel
25. Prier Jusqu'a Remporter La Victoire
26. Priere De Percees Pour Les Hommes D'affaires
27. Priere Pour Detruire Les Maladies Et Infirmites
28. Prieres Violentes Pour Humilier Les Problemes Opiniatres
29. Prieres De Comat Contre 70 Espirits Dechanines
30. Quand Les Choses Deviennent Difficiles
31. Que l'envoutement Perisse
32. Revoquer Les Decrets Malefiques
33. Se Liberer Des Alliances Malefiques
34. Ton Combat Et Ta Strategie

35. Victoires Sur Les Reves Sataniques
36. Votre Fondement Et Votre Destin

ANNUAL 70 DAYS PRAYER AND FASTING PUBLICATIONS

1. Prayers That Bring Miracles
2. Let God Answer By Fire
3. Prayers To Mount With Wings As Eagles
4. Prayers That Bring Explosive Increase
5. Prayers For Open Heavens
6. Prayers To Make You Fulfill Your Divine Destiny
7. Prayers That Make God To Answer And Fight By Fire
8. Prayers That Bring Unchallengeable Victory And Breakthrough Rainfall Bombardments
9. Prayers That Bring Dominion Prosperity And Uncommon Success
10. Prayers That Bring Power And Overflowing Progress
11. Prayers That Bring Laughter And Enlargement Breakthroughs
12. Prayers That Bring Uncommon Favour And Breakthroughs
13. Prayers That Bring Unprecedented Greatness And Unmatchable Increase
14. Prayers That Bring Awesome Testimonies And Turn Around Breakthroughs
15. Prayers That Bring Glorious Restoration
16. Prayers That Bring Unrivaled Lifting

1. Daughters of Philip
2. I Decree An Uncommon Change
3. Power To Fulfil Your Destiny
4. Principles of A Successful Marriage
5. The Call of God
6. When Your Destiny Is Under Attack
7. Woman of Wonder
8. Violence Against Negative Voices

**The Books, Tapes and CDs (Audio and Video)
All Obtainable At:**

☞ **Battle Cry Christian Ministries
322, Herbert Macaulay Way, Sabo, Yaba, Lagos
Phone: 01 8044415, 0803 304 4239**

☞ **MFM International Bookshop
13, Olasimbo Street, Onike, Yaba, Lagos**

☞ **MFM Prayer City
Km 12, Lagos/Ibadan Expressway**

☞ **54, Akeju Street, off Shipeolu Street
Palmgrove, Lagos**

☞ **All MFM Churches Nationwide**

☞ **All Leading Christian Bookstores**

31882402R00019

Made in the USA
San Bernardino, CA
22 March 2016